TIDINGS

Tidings

Don Gutteridge

Black Moss
Press
2015

Library and Archives Canada Cataloguing in Publication

Gutteridge, Don, 1937-, author
    Tidings / Don Gutteridge.

Poems.
ISBN 978-0-88753-551-2 (paperback)

    I. Title.

PS8513.U85T53 2015   C811'.54   C2015-903875-8

Cover photo by Marty Gervais
Layout & design by Jay Rankin
Edited by Meghan Desjardins

Published by Black Moss Press at 2450 Byng Road, Windsor, Ontario, N8W 3E8. Canada. Black Moss books are distributed in Canada and the U.S. by Fitzhenry & Whiteside. All orders should be directed there.

Fitzhenry & Whiteside
195 Allstate Parkway
Markham, ON
L3R 4T8

Black Moss would like to acknowledge the generous financial support from both the Canada Council for the Arts and the Ontario Arts Council.

I: THE WAY HOME

THE WAY HOME

The way home is thru
the heart, every blood-
beat hums with remembrance,
the village at the nub
of our being runs deep,
keeps our aloneness
at bay wherever
it finds us: estranged
as we are and listening
hard for that
emphatic thrum.

TIME WAS

Time was when Time
itself meant little:
the summer sun rose,
shone for a whole season
and settled in the welcoming
West, and all the while
we plied the ritual games
no rhyme or reason
could spy the end of,
or needed to, and swam
dolphin-eyed in the Great
Lake till evening
sank softly into it
with the promise of dawn
and another run with no
thought that Time was whittling
down the days one
              by one.

URGES

Who can ever forget
that sun-softened day
when we metamorphosed
into Fox and the Hounds,
across fields wild
with wheat and the unplumbed
depths of Leckie's Bush?
Intoxicated we were
by the chase, and like Hansel
and Gretel, grateful
for the paper spoor we tracked
like Comanches on a righteous
raid, and when the Fox
succumbed, we roused him
for fresh rounds of piracy
and the Cisco Kid:
forever reconciled
to the child-wise urges
in all of us.

MOVE UP

How many daylight
hours did we spend
on that vacant lot
playing our favourite
ungendered game?
Where the boy-girl divide
was rendered moot,
and anyone who could catch
a ball or cling to a
bat was free to move
up, was cheered and jeered
with equal ease, until
at last we deigned surrender
to the twilight shrouding
inexorably down
upon us whether
we willed it or not.

BITE

What I remember
most about those summer
days slung between June
and September is the feeling
of freedom at being
abruptly sprung from the
schoolyard in a daze
of jubilant release:
Tommy and I together
forever on the soothing dunes
of Canatara's beach,
where our sun-slaked
bodies lay length-
wise in their delight
and let the wavelets
of our imperturbable Lake
wash lovingly over us,
while Time itself paused
just long enough
to have us believe
it had no universal
                    bite.

MAGIC

Me just turned ten
and still believing
that Santa somehow
squeezed down our soot-
steeped chimney and landed
foot-first and noiseless
on the living room rug,
a sack of goodies bulging
on his back; no matter that
they looked suspiciously
like the ones we'd spied
in the five-and-dime the day
before: magic is a
wonder hard to give up,
and toys are toys.

GRIEF

The night I first heard
my father cry: a single
anguished utterance,
the Earth tilted on its axis
half an inch or more,
and I thought of the oak
sturdy in our yard bent to
breaking in a tormenting wind,
and everything I'd known
and trusted was suddenly
as fragile as the life
of my dying grandfather,
and grief was a live being
with little time for childish
tears.

HOME-GROWN

My village made me
what I came to be:
the curve of Canatara's
bountiful beach,
the infinite surge
of Huron Lake, the marshes
below the angular Bridge
spanning the blue
cadence of our River,
while meadows bounced
with bobolinks near a park
where we played until
the evening evaporated –
these were all of God's
geography I would need
to track the terrain of a story
or the swerve of a poem
with my cartographer's eye,
or people them with characters
even Dickens would die for:
home-grown and in-
advertently comic,
they acted out the minor
flaws of their little lives
as if I were the only one
watching, and beguiling
the village air with my
grateful applause.

GALILEE

For a hundred Sundays
and more, I became
acquainted with God, His Son
and the blood of the Lamb (of which
we were all washed clean),
with lurid tales of Adam
and Eve rambunctious in Eden,
with Zacharias trembling
in a tree, with luckless saints
who beat the odds and the
occasional flood, with David
whose pious pebble bested
Goliath, with Samson's
plucky locks in Delilah's
severing scissors,
and of course with Jesus
pinned horrific on
Golgotha: images that
fired my fancy and drew
me, dazzled, out of my way-
ward village ten
thousand miles from
                    Galilee.

HUNTING

Dad fits me up
with a sixteen-gauge
("Easier on the shoulder," he says)
and cracks his twelve-gauge
with a military snap.
Dutifully I follow him
into our neighbour's winter
woods, trying not to step
into those huge footprints,
and looking out for unwary
rabbits cowering
in every hedge and brush-
pile, out of which a foolish
cottontail springs
in time to take a blast
from my father's steady gun.
I watch its life ease
out of it, one cold eye
staring straight up
as if the sky had an answer,
and then there's its mate
rabbiting into the open.
"Shoot!" my father says,
and I pull the trigger,
knowing even then
that I would raise the sight
an inch too high.
"You missed," Dad says,
trying his best to believe
I have really tried

BELONGING

When I think of the place
where I was born and ushered
into the world without ceremony,
I remember snow
falling as softly
as the Babe's breath in a
manger ten thousand
miles away, and no
breeze to blemish such
perfection, and I let
it drift upon my face
(uplifted to the Heavens)
like a benediction on
                    belonging.

SOME THINGS

At precisely ten after six
every Saturday evening,
just past closing
time at the Balmoral,
Bob McCord staggered
past our house, singing
off-key and entertaining
the street all along his way-
ward route; we'd watch
him enter his front door
and stumble into silence,
after which came the slap
heard round the village.
And sometime later
Mrs. McCord would appear
on her front porch as if
nothing had happened,
smiling grimly at those
unashamed enough
to pass by, and young
though I was, I thought:
this is the way things are
in our town, and then:
there are some things
that shouldn't be.

DESIRES

Whenever the good
reverend mentioned
Heaven, I pictured
Elijah's fiery rise
or Jacob's leavening
ladder, while Cherubim
chuckled like oversize
babies and angels
provoked applause
at the Pearly Gates, and no-
one dare allow
that Satan stood just
beyond the hallowed
walls, stoking
          our desires.

BRAVERY

I was afraid of bees
before they were born
each spring out of their
cozy combs, the hum
of a drone reconnoitring
a daffodil would send
my heart drumming with the
thrill of a fear so
primal I found
no words to give it
a name, and that time
in First Bush when my handle-
bar brushed a hive
and a hundred barb-
tipped dive-bombers
spun free, I
staggered home, sobbing,
stung from stem to stern,
but Gran called me brave,
and in my endless innocence
I believed her.

THE DAY I ALMOST DROWNED

The day I almost drowned
was an ordinary summer's
afternoon, the sun
soothing the rough waters
around the village pier,
when for a dime or a dare
I offered to circum-
navigate the jetty,
and set about the challenge
with a will and a reckless
paddling, and almost
made it to the cheers
from the shoreline, when
out of nowhere I felt
a chuck under my chin
and a strong arm guiding
me, against my better
judgement, un-
ceremoniously to safety,
where I sat dazed
and thinking only that
I would remember this
as the day I almost
                    drowned.

EASTER SUNDAY

When I think of Easter
I think not of Christ
stretched upon His cross
nor of that stubborn stone
miraculously rolled
away, but rather recall
a long-ago Sunday
when morning bloomed with
sunshine and church bells
tolled the faithful home,
and a ten-year-old boy
skipped the cracks in his grand-
mother's sidewalk
and hummed some Sunday
school ditty learned
by heart and singing
now within as if Jesus
and all His world were real.

THE LAKE OF MY CHILDHOOD

When I was eleven
I learned for good
I wasn't a dolphin,
thru the svelte waves of Huron
I burrowed and flailed
like a walrus without a tail,
there was no daring
in the dives I mistook
once the rollers had slowed,
I felt only fear
as I stood and shook
on the pier's edge while my
buddies cannon-balled
and belly-flopped as if
they'd been born with fins
and a rudder; even today
I cannot pass the Great
Lake of my childhood
without a nod and modicum
of shudder.

PLEASURE

For Kenny Waters

Kenny and I diving
for bottlecaps in the shallows
of the sea-deep Lake:
Pepsi, Coke, Orange
Crush – a treasure trove
of logos we dove after
in dolphin-eyed tandem
under a simmering sun,
while Huron held us in its
wombed vise, twinned
in mutual pleasure.

WORKSHOP

Fifty-five years
since you left us, and still
I see you in your Saturday
morning workshop, bent
over the lathe like a lover
his beloved, curling square
steel for the whirligigs
you peopled our village with;
I remember it all as fresh
as yesterday with a tremulous
eye and a hurt heart.

IN THE SWEET BYE AND BYE

Bob and I: alone
in our room, he carolling
"In the Sweet Bye and Bye"
with its promise of mansions
so fair, and I: enthralled
in its singsong innocence.

Bob and I: apart now
for half a lifetime,
yet sometimes I hear
him singing still:
Won't it be glorious
when we get there?

II: HERE AND NOW

STORY

For Katie-Ann

My granddaughter watching
Dora the Explorer, absorbed
by story, her body tuned
to every twist and turn
of the tale, the prototypal
three-act drama
complete with villain
and treasure map,
and a plot as old and deep
as her dreams.

FRIENDSHIP

For Alvin Gehl

You were always too old
for your age, ever the little
man even when you were just
a lad under your mother's
imperious thumb;
you let me be myself
at a time when I wasn't sure
what that was, quick to forgive
and loyal to a fault; I think
of you often and regret
the years I allowed to ease
between us; I wish
you well wherever you are.

FOR MY GRANDMOTHER

When grandfather died
your world was abruptly halved,
all those little rituals
that bound you one to one
now ended, you could not bear
ever again to sleep
in the bed you shared for more
than fifty years, your dreams
entangled through the long night
until morning woke you
with a new day; I remember
you best in the evenings,
you knitting in the kitchen,
Gramps snoozing through the news
a room away, but both of you
linked by love.

GLORY

*On Watching James
Play Football*

These bantam paladins
clash in a brutal ballet
of choreographed violence
played out on an innocent
checkerboard stage:
in their daring and dashing, these
fourteen-year-old
bodies harbour the heroic
and grapple for glory.

REBECCA READS

Rebecca pretends to read,
the book open on her lap:
the lips move as if animated
by the plight of the Three Bears
and she utters a headlong
singsong chant
as if propelled by the lustrous
letters on the page, as if
some rudimentary story
has already lodged pell-
mell in her bright, child-
lit mind.

HESITATION

Moon over Bethlehem:
a lonely stranger,
its ghostly glow on loft
and manger where the Babe lies
open to the air and to the star-
lit skies where angels
breathe their benediction
and all the world below
hesitates ...

INSIDE

Outside the blizzard's
descent is relentless,
its pent fury smothers
eave and edge, etches
the trees' stark filigree,
diminishes any horizon
in a blind obliteration,
in a whirligig of white,
and somewhere at the storm's
nub is a dark deeper
than dark, while inside,
cocooned by snow, the heart
grows inward, dreams
of Easter's sun willing
the world green.

ALWAYS

When I'll no longer be,
the world will while away
the hours with someone
other than me, and what
I've left behind – a few
scattered words worth
repeating and a handful
of loved ones I touched
here and there over
the long years of my life –
these things will soon
matter no more than
my foolish desire
to dwell among the living.
Now and always.

HOW OFTEN

How often as I edge
into my age do I think
of that long-ago night
when shepherds, anchored
to the Earth, sat bolt
upright on their snow-
brushed hillside
and hearkened to the Good News,
while in the distant desert
Magi rolled west-
ward, stunned by a star
drawing them to a faraway
manger where a Bethlehem
Babe is born to tempt
the world out of its wilderness.

HOPEFUL

More and more I think
about those long-ago
Sundays when we sang
our salvation
and Heaven rested
just above the steeple's
infinite reach,
O how we rang the rafters
with the "Blood of the Lamb"
and "Jesus Loves Me,"
praying in our hopeful
hearts that God does
see the sparrow fall,
that somewhere beyond
our sequestered selves
another life lies
           waiting.

ALLIES

Nothing abides like love:
for fifty-odd years
side by side we have
weathered the world and not
grown weary, two
souls allied as one
since that moment so
long ago when we eyed
one another and satisfied
something wistful
inside; and here, now,
riding out our last days,
we smile and, knowingly,
                              nod.

TUNDRA SWANS AT GRAND BEND

Out of the blue they swoop
like a squadron of B-52s,
defying gravity, and cruise
to a stealthy stop on the
welcoming water,
and in the late-winter air
a thousand winnowing
wings are furled: a triumph
of instinct over reason,
as every March they home in
upon this pat Canadian
pond to rest a while
before hurling themselves
Heavenward once more
on their way towards the far
Tundra that gives them
their name.

PLOTS

I was the boy who told
himself stories, lisping
them half-aloud in the
schoolyard, risking
ridicule or worse
for the sake of some urging
I could not do without:
the need to wonder-weave
fanciful plots
and peaceable endings,
tales of callow courage
and daring-do that gave
me more joy than Heaven-
and-Earth usually allow.

THANKFUL

I'd like to thank whoever
it is who arranges
the cosmic doings
of this Universe, for it would
have been just as convenient,
when I was seven and struck
down with rheumatic fever,
to have let my fractured heart
slip quietly into oblivion,
but it didn't, and I'd like
to think that it was I who chose
life, when it was actually
life who chose me and all
that followed.

TIDINGS

On that first Christmas
so long ago
shepherds contended
with their flocks on wind-weathered
and forlorn hillside,
when the skies opened up
and glowed golden
and Gabriel blew
his heraldic horn
and let such tidings
ride his music to the far
Heavens that they knew
in their hearts something
glorious had happened
to the world and all its
                    urges.

ELEMENTAL

It's hard to believe
in your own demise:
something precious and
elemental inside us
resists the temptation
to un-be, to picture
that moment when nothing
comes after, when the last
syllable's expressed
and the long monologue
of our life is over;
O it's hard not to believe
our words will carry on
regardless.

DREAMING

I wake up still
dreaming of Nancy,
the girl I idolized
when I was barely
eleven, and could find no
words to sanctify my feelings
about one who fuelled
my fancy with a single
glance whenever I
dared meet those
forbidding eyes,
and I wonder yet
at the pubescent power
of such dreaming, then
and now.

INKLING

I stroll into the garden
and something in the hush
of it stirs a chill
I cannot quell
nor wish to, something
there is in the lushness
of these blooms, a teeming
of tulip and daffodil:
an alien inkling
of what is unwilling
to be anything
other than itself,
an intimation of what
cannot, quite, be known,
that brings us to the brink
and leaves us there
dreaming of what might
                    have been.

STASIS

Whenever I think of the
slow drift of my body
towards death and its final
stasis, I dream of those
days when the morning sun
seasoned everything
it touched and made it glow
for my eyes only,
when the air renewed itself
each noon so that I
might savour its subtle
sifting and feel again
the throb of being alive
in a world fashioned
just for me, when the days
passed by with the ease
of breathing, and I had
no reason to wonder
                why

COURAGE

No better man
braved the battlegrounds
of Belgium, that blighted
ruin, than my grandfather:
criss-crossing for
almost four years
the maelstrom of No
Man's Land no man
could survive a minute in
when the stuttering gunneries
loosed their havoc upon
the poppy fields and ground
them to floundering muck,
three times wounded
he somehow survived,
calling on the great god
Luck and the deepest drive
within us: the courage
                    to be.

FANCY

When I was first eleven
I spun my stories
out of an elfin alphabet,
created a whole kingdom
of characters who danced
in my dreams and persuaded
my pen across the page
through the daylight hours
I fuelled with my fancy,
and did not guess, even then,
a lifelong pursuit of poems
and tales and the fabular
world we inhabit
when the gods aren't looking.

THE LINK

Alvin, my boyhood pal,
is on the phone wanting to know
if I remember Walter
who owned the beet farm
just west of Chatham,
and instantly I am back-
wards in time and wielding
a short-handled hoe
among the thistled beets,
Alvin beside me as row
upon row we move in tandem,
not knowing the link we forged
there in a farmer's field
would last a lifetime.

III: MISCELLANY

GRASPING AT LOVE

The heart is ever an exile,
no matter how much
we strive to render it free
of longing and loneliness:
though the mind reach out
to touch the tendrils of another,
it cannot bridge the gaping
gap between, while grasping
at love as if it might ex-
foliate and leave the heart
harmonious.

ABSENCE

It's impossible to miss
what we already have,
we can't imagine absence
any more than we can wish
ourselves other than
what we are, thus
we cling to what
is already and still
within our grasp, hoping
against hope that love
                        will last.

LOSING YOU

For Uncle Potsy, in memoriam

You built your own
house, block by cinder
block, you levelled them
with an eye as keen as a
cartographer's and a mind
that could calculate angles
and eaves as precise
as a prism, you put
no stock in new-
fangled gadgets, relying
only on the heft and timbre
of your woodman's hands,
and the home-built structure
stood for fifty years until
they bulldozed it for a parking
lot. And I pass that
vacant space now
as if what you created
had never been there
for most of a lifetime,
and, like losing you,
I feel bereft.

THE GATHERING

Friends since school days,
you gather faithfully
each September to break
bread (lovingly prepared)
and remember the when
and where of lives lived
jointly and apart, keen
to re-tell the stories
you've heard a dozen times
and prize even more because
the years slip away
and there will come a moment
when there are no Septembers
left to celebrate,
with tears and laughter,
the love and communion
you have felt for one
another all these
                    years.

MEMORY

There is nothing wrong
with growing old (try
as we might to capture
again those rare days
when life allowed us
a momentary triumph
or two) but memories
are no substitute
for the flesh-and-blood
aliveness of things
we long to reprise
but can't, though we seize
every chance we can
conjure to cling
to their fast-fading
hopefulness.

TALENT

For my father, in memoriam

My Dad, dead at
fifty-seven, the whiskey
he so wilfully sipped
thru the delicate lip
of his kidney finally
stilled: this youth
who wielded a hockey stick
like a conductor's baton
and dazzled the crowd
with skating as intricate
as a jazzman's riffs;
this father who could hit
a bullseye at thirty
paces or mortar a seam
of bricks as perfect as a
surveyor's sighting,
who taught himself
taxidermy and mounted
bighorn sheep
in Alberta's foothills,
who could croon like Crosby
or dance like Astaire,
who was good at everything
except saving himself.

AN ODD THOUGHT

Woke up with an odd
thought buffeting my brain:
"I am now an old man"
huffing and puffing my way
to breakfast, no longer
growing old gracefully
or merely getting on
in years, and I think
such a thought could kill
me at my age.

HOPE

The world is multiple
and no one thing
is quite like another,
the rose does not repeat
its variable bloom,
each leaf resists
concentricity
and makes room for a thousand
thousand brothers, and so
it is, we hug what we have
and harrow hope for the rest.

BRAVING THE ODDS

It's a long way home
wherever you happen to be,
the past is always past
whatever we happen
to remember in the long
days of our aloneness,
the memory can't outlast
the fleeting grasp we have
of it, but home is what
the heart craves, and so
in God's good time
we hearken there,
braving the odds
whenever we can.

ARRIVAL

Like clockwork they come
each April in the morning:
orioles in the new-sprung
leafage, their song
as pleasantly piercing
as a mezzo-soprano's
soaring serenade,
their perfect punctuality
and airy arias oddly
reassuring in a world
otherwise random.

TEACHER

For Geoffrey Millburn, in memoriam

How many teachers
do you know who could call
their students "miserable wretches"
and have them smile as if
some benediction
had floated down upon
them? But that was the man,
quick of wit, sharp-
tongued whenever a gerund
or comma got misplaced,
editor extraordinaire,
a professional curmudgeon
who played that game, and many
others, well, and if there's
somewhere a God of Grammar,
Geoff will smile and say,
"All's right with the world!"

CHARACTER

Lucky was I to be born
in a place where character
was more than a word: up
and down the village streets
Dickensian lookalikes
danced to the tantalizing
tunes in their head, and, shorn
of all pretension, acted out
their vivid lives for the one
watching, mesmerized,
in the wings – pen poised.

THE GARDEN

Adam was the first gardener,
they say, gouging the gaunt
earth with his home-made
plough and cursing the God
who tossed him headlong
out of Eden, where the groves
grew lush in the lustrous
light of the savouring sun
and the corn sprung of its own
accord, and Eve waxed
lovely, unadorned
and unavid for apples
or fornicating asps.

But the fruit got bitten
and here they are:
coupled and care-worn,
pitted against an un-
bending world, and tending
the garden of their own making.

ARTICULATE

As I ease into my age,
content with those gifts
the Gods have graced to me,
I hearken back to beginnings:
that lucid lunge for air,
my lungs bursting with their
first word: a howl
that would be the prolonged
poem of my life, by which
I would voice a thousand
thoughts – rhymed and ready
to make the unwilling
world
      articulate.

GONE

If I were gone and worlds
away, would anyone
weep or say he was a
fine fellow who whittled
words and gloried in stories,
whose worth was a little more
than little? Would my grandchildren
in their age still keep
me in their heart of hearts,
or will the memory of who
I was or sought to be
lie, like all the others,
fallow and unfurled?

I THINK OF YOU

For my brother Bob, in memoriam

I think of you trussed
up in that hospital
with all the indignities
of modern medicine
thrust upon you,
keeping you a hair's
breadth from death,
and I wonder if you dreamt
of those days of our shared
boyhood and how
I admired what those
talented hands could do
and how your ears echoed
with the sea-sound of
symphonies and how
your fingers coaxed
each brushstroke
across the reluctant canvas,
and I pray you passed
peacefully into a place
where there is no pain.

SAID AND DONE

There will be time, when all
is said and done, for the rictus
of regret, and time, when wishes
are all that we pictured,
to realize we never reached
those skies high enough
to risk a fall or compro-
mise our pet convictions,
and time to find the rhyme
or reason for what has fled
our envying grasp,
when all is done and said.

HARMONY

For Anne and for John Barnett, in memoriam

Some days before he died
Anne fetched her father
from the tedium of his nursing home,
put him in a taxi
(wheelchair and all)
and together they motored
back through the village
John had known for more
than half his life, each
house precisely familiar,
jogging memories as they flashed
by, and as soon as the Lake
came into view, they paused,
and easefully Anne manoeuvred
the chair down to the beach
and side by side they sat
and stared out at the
calming waters, father
and daughter locked
in mutual harmony,
sharing all that had passed
and what was left of their
                                future.